BLAZERS

To the Extreme

Motocross Racing

By Mandy R. Marx

Reading Consultant:
Barbara J. Fox
Reading Specialist
North Carolina State University

Capstone
press

Mankato, Minnesota

Blazers is published by Capstone Press,
151 Good Counsel Drive, P.O. Box 669, Mankato, Minnesota 56002.
www.capstonepress.com

Library of Congress Cataloging-in-Publication Data
Marx, Mandy.
   Motocross racing / by Mandy R. Marx.
   p. cm.—(Blazers. To the extreme)
   Includes bibliographical references and index.
   ISBN-13: 978-0-7368-5462-7 (hardcover)
   ISBN-10: 0-7368-5462-2 (hardcover)
   1. Motocross—Juvenile literature. I. Title. II. Series.
GV1060.12.M37 2006
796.7'56—dc22   2005020092

Summary: Discusses the sport of motocross racing, including
   equipment used, safety, and competitions.

Editorial Credits
Carrie A. Braulick, editor; Jason Knudson, set designer; Kate
   Opseth and Jenny Bergstrom, book designers; Wanda Winch,
   photo researcher; Scott Thoms, photo editor

Photo Credits
Frank Hoppen, cover, 6, 11, 15, 16–17, 19, 20, 24
Getty Images Inc, Steve Bruhn, 27
Steve Bruhn, 5, 7, 9, 13, 14, 23, 28–29

This book is dedicated to the memory of Curt Braulick.

1 2 3 4 5 6 11 10 09 08 07 06

Table of Contents

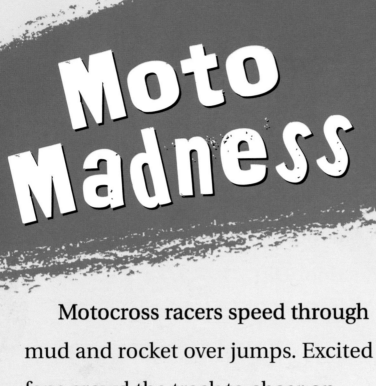

Moto Madness

Motocross racers speed through mud and rocket over jumps. Excited fans crowd the track to cheer on their favorite racers.

The racers weave through the course, leaving behind clouds of dust. They round corners on steep banks of dirt called berms.

Berm

Double

BLAZER FACT

A double is two jumps placed close together.

Fans cheer as the final lap ends. Only seconds separate the winner from the racer in last place.

BLAZER FACT

A dirt bike's engine size is measured in cubic centimeters (cc). Most racers have 125cc or 250cc engines.

Designed for Dirt

Motocross bikes are called dirt bikes. They are built to ride on rough terrain.

Dirt bike tires have knobs
called treads. The treads grip
the muddy track.

BLAZER FACT

Lightweight frames help
dirt bikes reach top
speeds of 75 miles
(121 kilometers) per hour.

Tires spray dirt as they rip up the track. Fenders and exhaust pipes sit up high, so they won't scrape the ground or get clogged with mud.

Dirt Bike Diagram

Back fender

Exhaust pipe

Tire treads

Engine

Handlebars

Front fender

Shock absorber

Motocross Safety

Motocross racers are bound to take a tumble now and then. Safety equipment helps protect them from injuries.

Helmet

Body armor

Boot

Racers wear helmets, sturdy boots, and body armor. With this gear, racers focus on the finish line instead of worrying about crashing.

BLAZER FACT

In 2005, Utah's governor made the second week of April "Motocross Safety Week."

Pro Racing

Becoming a professional motocross racer takes hard work. Racers practice for years to become pros.

Fans from around the world are wild about pro racing. Motorcycle organizations sponsor pro races in the United States, Canada, and Europe.

BLAZER FACT

The first major motocross race took place in France in 1947. It was called Motocross des Nations.

Pro motocross events have two races, or motos. The top 20 racers of each moto earn points. The racer with the most points wins the event.

Mud and guts!

Glossary

berm (BURM)—a banked turn or corner on a motocross track

body armor (BOD-ee AR-mur)—a plastic shield with foam lining that motocross racers wear to protect their chests

fender (FEN-dur)—a covering over a dirt bike wheel that protects the wheel from damage

moto (MOH-toh)—a single motocross race; each motocross event includes two motos.

sponsor (SPON-sur)—to give money and support to people putting on an event

terrain (tuh-RAYN)—the surface of the land

Read More

Blomquist, Christopher. *Motocross in the X Games.* A Kid's Guide to the X Games. New York: PowerKids Press, 2003.

Doeden, Matt. *Dirt Bikes.* Horsepower. Mankato, Minn.: Capstone Press, 2005.

Poolos, J. *Travis Pastrana: Motocross Superstar.* Extreme Sports Biographies. New York: Rosen Central, 2005.

Internet Sites

FactHound offers a safe, fun way to find Internet sites related to this book. All of the sites on FactHound have been researched by our staff.

Here's how:

1. Visit *www.facthound.com*
2. Type in this special code **0736854622** for age-appropriate sites. Or enter a search word related to this book for a more general search.
3. Click on the **Fetch It** button.

FactHound will fetch the best sites for you!

Index